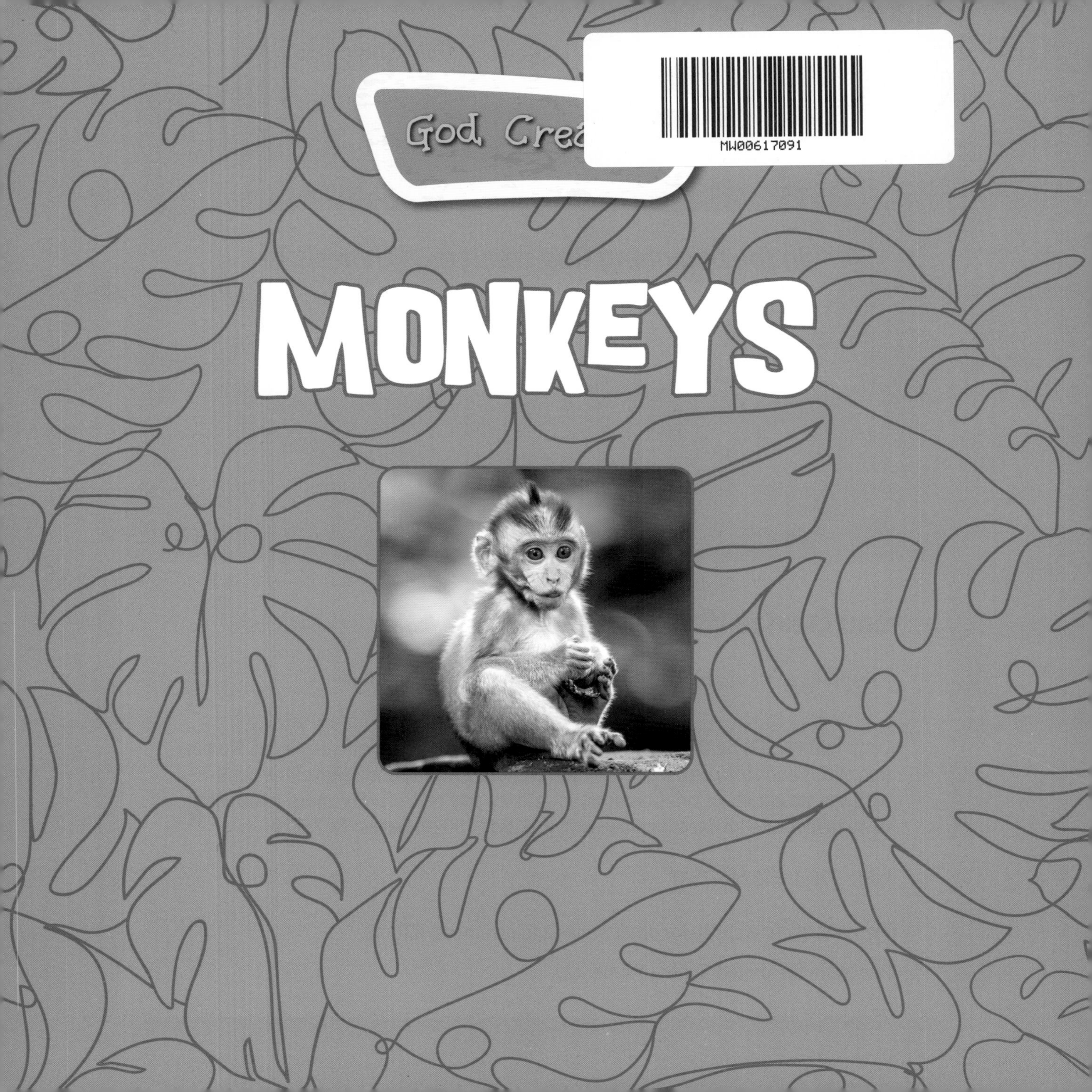
MONKEYS
MW00617091

"In the beginning God created..." Genesis 1:1

God Created Monkeys

First printing: November 2021

ISBN: 978-1-946246-75-2

Please visit our website for other books and resources: ICR.org

Printed in the United States of America.

MONKEYS

INSTITUTE FOR CREATION RESEARCH
Dallas, TX
ICR.org

WHAT IS A MONKEY

Who doesn't love to monkey around sometimes? But what makes a monkey, well...a monkey? Monkeys fit into a scientific group called primates. Primates are hairy creatures with forward-facing eyes, and hands and feet that can hold things. That means gorillas and chimpanzees are in the primate group, too. But gorillas and chimpanzees are apes, not monkeys.

Vervet Monkey

Chimpanzee (ape)

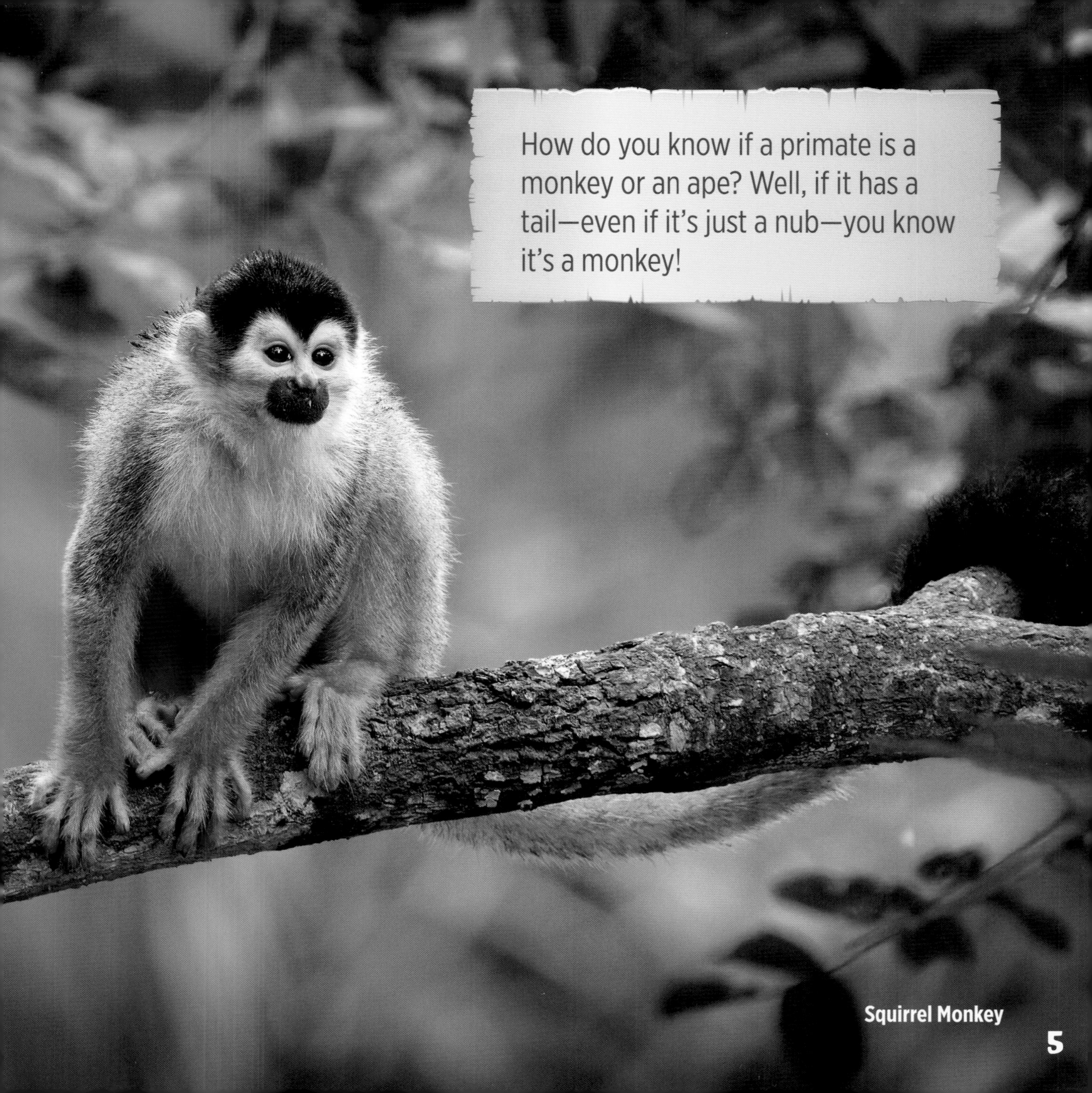

How do you know if a primate is a monkey or an ape? Well, if it has a tail—even if it's just a nub—you know it's a monkey!

Squirrel Monkey

MONKEYS WERE CREATED

So where did monkeys come from? The Lord Jesus created monkeys and other land animals on Day 6 of the creation week. The Bible tells us that's also the same day He created the first people, Adam and Eve.

Genesis 1:27 says that "God created man in His own image...male and female He created them." Monkeys are amazing creatures. But they will never have the image of God like you do!

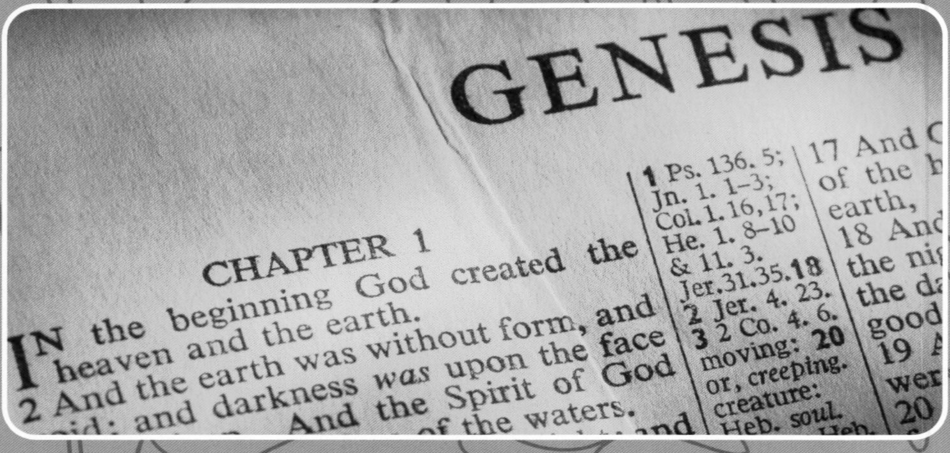

SIX DAYS OF CREATION

DAY 1

DAY 2

DAY 3

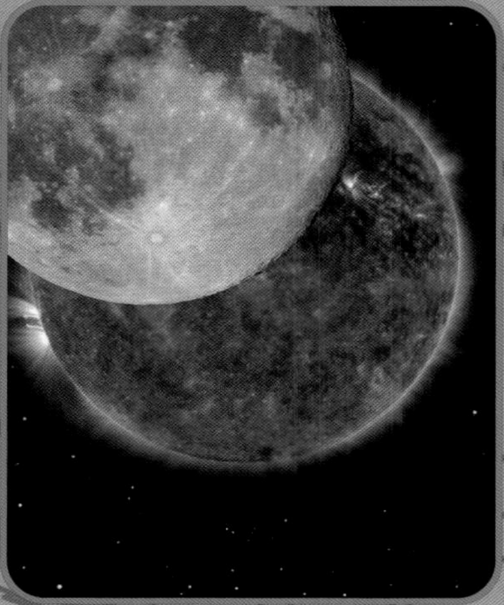

DAY 4

DAY 5

DAY 6

OLD WORLD MONKEY SPECIES

There are over 250 different species of monkeys. The species that came from Europe, Africa, and Asia are known as Old World monkeys.

Old World monkeys spend more time on the ground and can't use their tails for much. However, they do have thick pads on their bottoms. This extra padding makes them more comfortable while they sit on the ground.

Blue Monkey

Golden Snub-Nosed Monkey

Toque Macaque

NEW WORLD MONKEY SPECIES

Monkeys from North and South America are called New World monkeys.

New World monkeys live mostly in trees. They can usually hold onto objects with their tails. Their tails also help them balance as they scamper through the trees.

Isn't it awesome how Jesus created animals with the features they need to thrive where they live?

Bearded Emperor Tamarin

Silvery Marmoset

Howler Monkey

WHO'S WHO IN THE MONKEY WORLD

The smallest monkey, the pygmy marmoset, can fit in the palm of a human hand.

You can hear the howler monkey's loud calls from three miles away.

Baboons display a dog-like muzzle, and they can't grasp objects with their tails.

The Longest Tail Award goes to the female spider monkey.

The proboscis monkey has a funny face, and it's the best swimmer!

Mandrills, with their colorful faces, are the largest monkeys in the world.

MONKEY HAIRSTYLES

Jesus designed animals to display incredible variety within their kinds. Their features can be beautiful and majestic, somewhat strange, or even downright funny. Check out these fashionably fun monkey hairstyles!

Cotton-Top Tamarin

Golden Lion Tamarin

Marmoset

Titi Monkey

Emperor Tamarin

Crested Black Macaque

Toque Macaque

Gelada Baboon

Monkey Skills

Some monkeys have special skills. In the wild, the capuchin monkey uses leaves like gloves, catches food with tools, and hits snakes with large branches!

Capuchins can also be trained to do simple tasks for people who have physical disabilities. These monkeys live in their owner's home and pick up objects, turn pages, scratch itches, and push buttons or switches for phones, computers, TVs, and more.

Capuchin

THE NUTCRACKER

Some capuchin monkeys live in dry regions of Brazil where food is harder to find. So they mainly eat nuts with very hard shells. How do they crack them open? They slam heavy rocks on top of the nuts.

Scientists think capuchins may have learned this trick from watching humans many centuries ago. It's hard work for only a bit of food. And it can take three years for a capuchin to become an expert nutcracker.

MONKEY MUNCHIES

What else do monkeys eat? It might surprise you to learn that they don't normally eat bananas. They *can* eat them, but most bananas don't grow in the wild—they have to be planted.

Monkeys are omnivores. That means they eat both plants and meat. A healthy monkey diet often includes fruits, seeds, leaves, and flowers. Some monkeys even eat bird eggs, insects, and other small animals.

Squirrel Monkey

Macaque Monkey

Macaque Monkey

Golden Lion Tamarin

Long-Tailed Macaque

FAMILY MATTERS

When a monkey is born, its mom nurses and cares for it for four to seven months. Baby monkeys often ride on their mom's back or hang from her neck.

Stump-Tailed Macaque

Dusky Leaf Monkey

Gray Langur

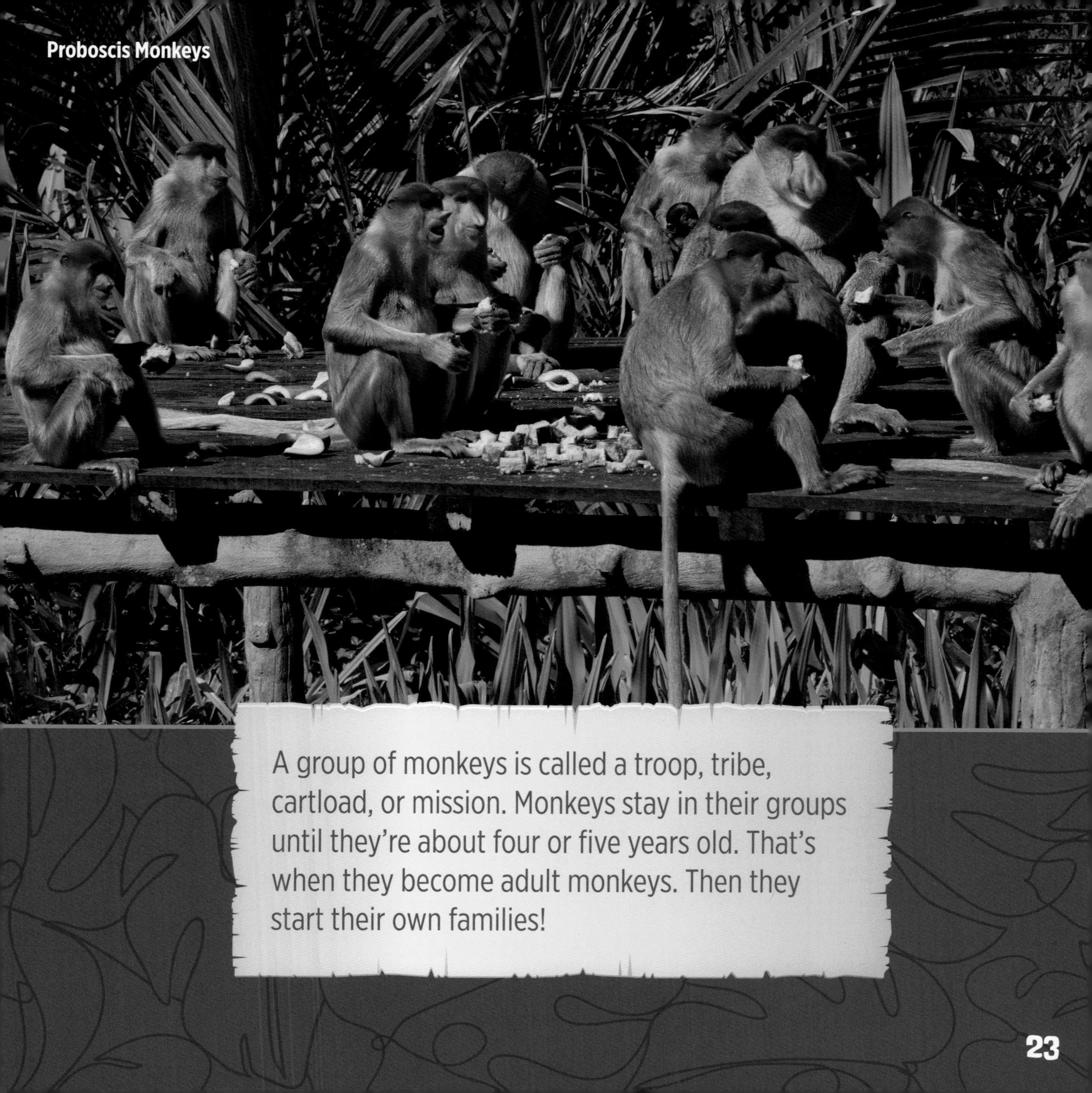

A group of monkeys is called a troop, tribe, cartload, or mission. Monkeys stay in their groups until they're about four or five years old. That's when they become adult monkeys. Then they start their own families!

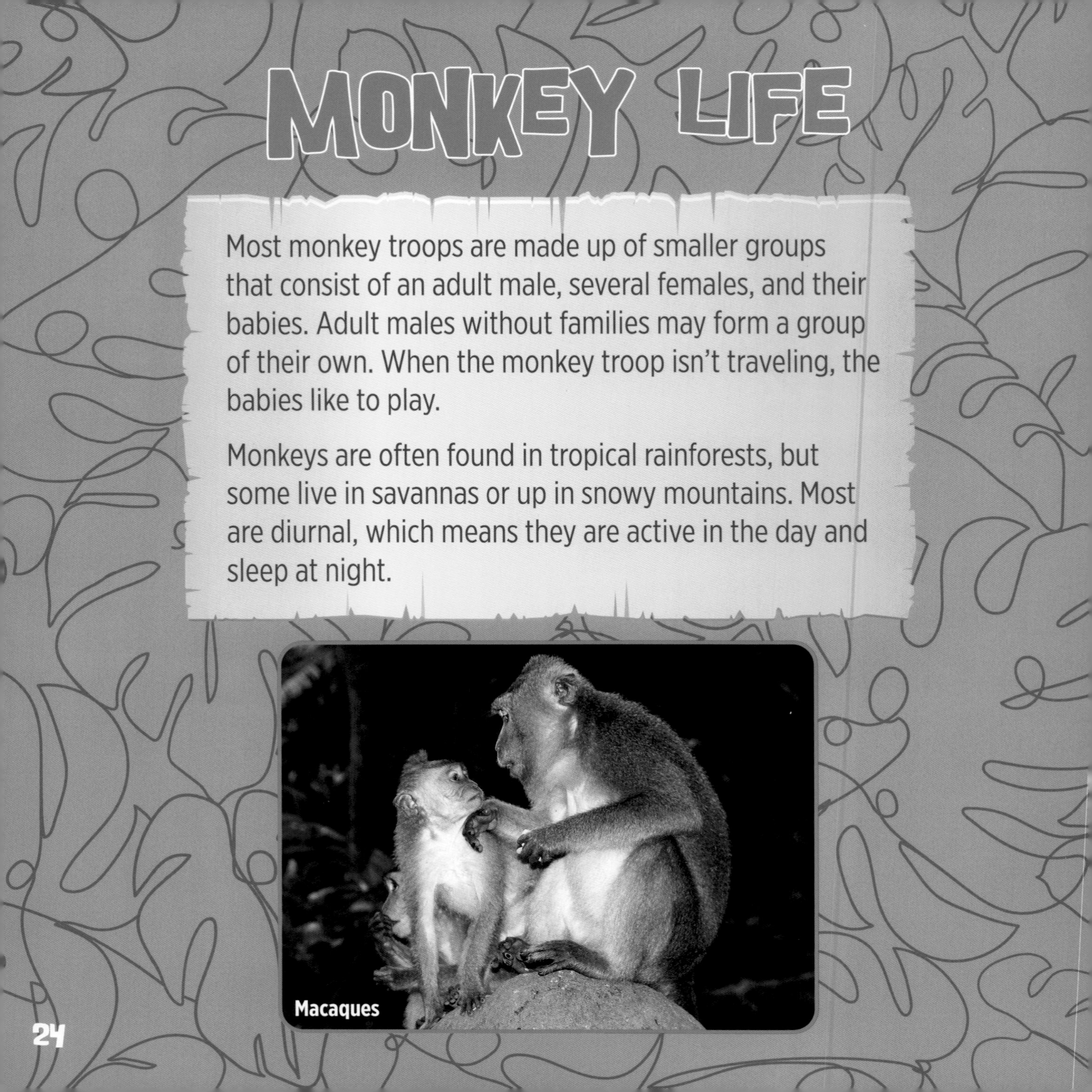

MONKEY LIFE

Most monkey troops are made up of smaller groups that consist of an adult male, several females, and their babies. Adult males without families may form a group of their own. When the monkey troop isn't traveling, the babies like to play.

Monkeys are often found in tropical rainforests, but some live in savannas or up in snowy mountains. Most are diurnal, which means they are active in the day and sleep at night.

Macaques

Snow Monkeys
Gelada Baboons

Macaques

MONKEY TALK

Monkeys bark, scream, grunt, squeak, hoot, wail, and moan to communicate. A monkey will sometimes bare its teeth and look like it's smiling. But don't be fooled! That actually means it's angry. Monkeys also stare to threaten each other. The other monkey looks away if it wants to avoid a fight.

Monkeys know how to make friends, too. They show affection by grooming each other, twisting their tails together, and smacking their lips.

Crab-Eating Macaque

Mandrill

Diana Monkey

Barbary Macaques

MONKEYS DID NOT EVOLVE

Evolution scientists think an unknown creature that lived millions of years ago slowly turned into monkeys, apes (such as chimpanzees), and humans. They think this happened through small changes over time.

But there are too many differences between humans, monkeys, and chimps and other apes for that to have happened. Even many millions of years would not be enough time! God created people as people, and monkeys as monkeys, and apes as apes.

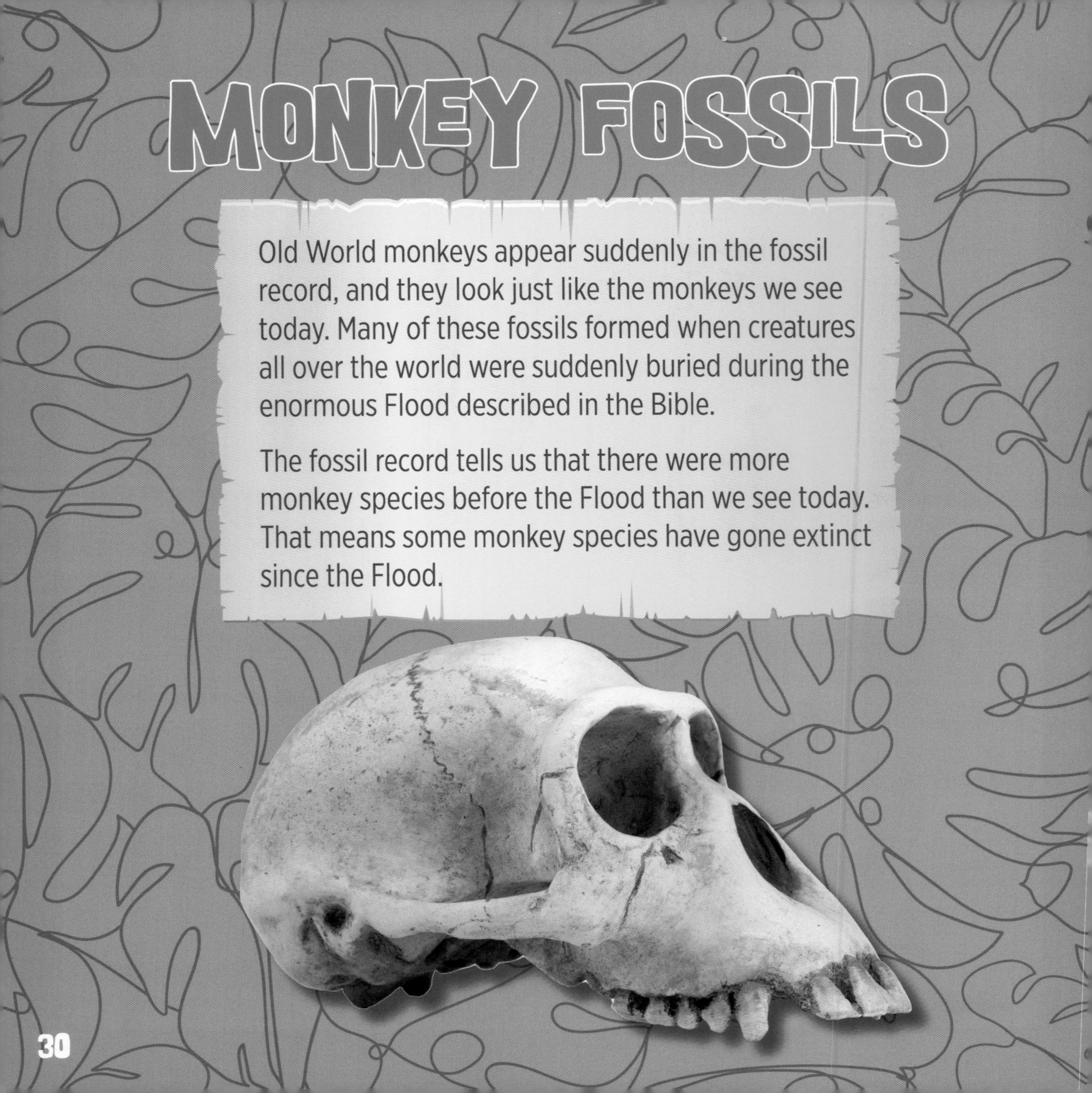

MONKEY FOSSILS

Old World monkeys appear suddenly in the fossil record, and they look just like the monkeys we see today. Many of these fossils formed when creatures all over the world were suddenly buried during the enormous Flood described in the Bible.

The fossil record tells us that there were more monkey species before the Flood than we see today. That means some monkey species have gone extinct since the Flood.

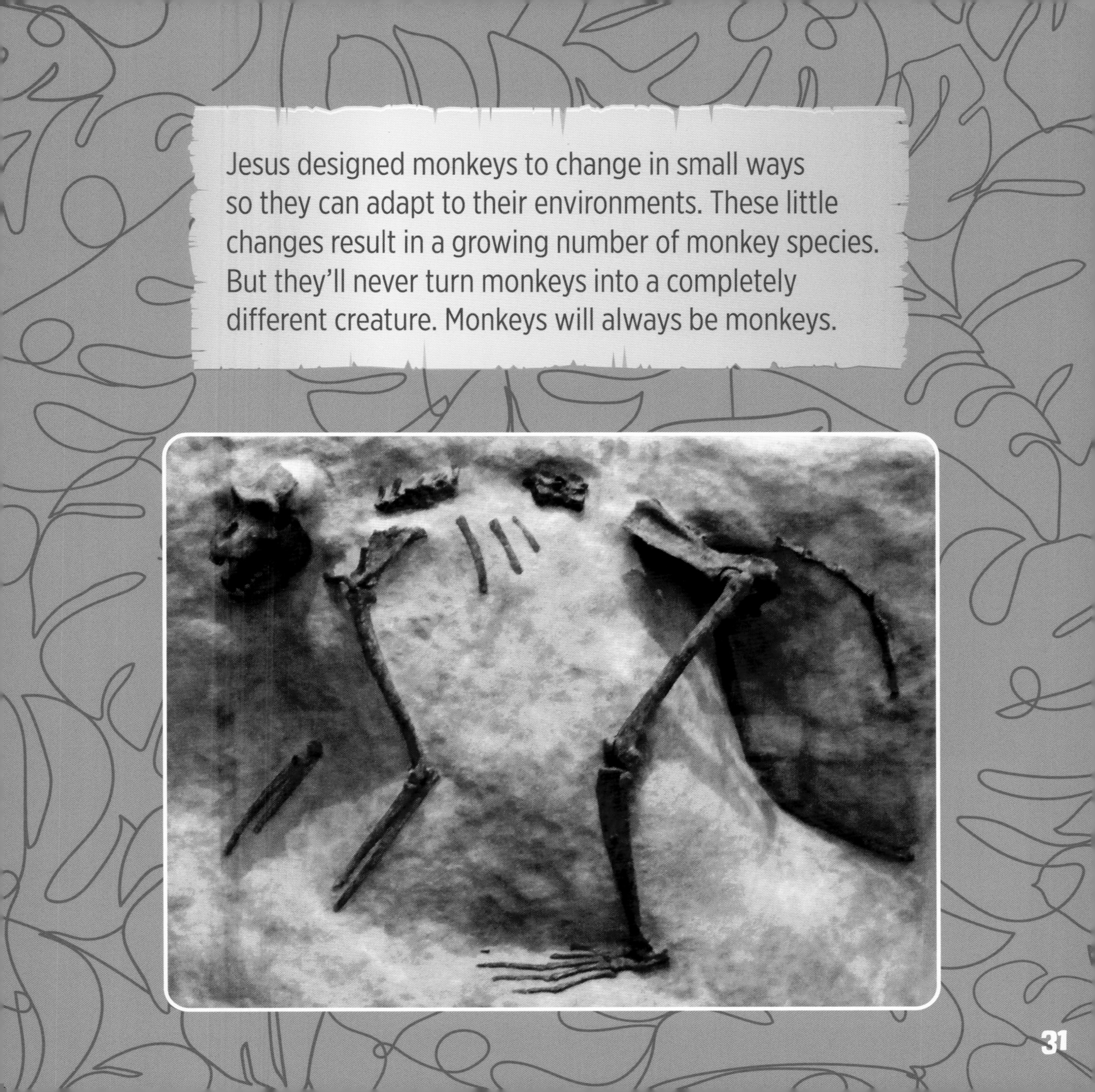

Jesus designed monkeys to change in small ways so they can adapt to their environments. These little changes result in a growing number of monkey species. But they'll never turn monkeys into a completely different creature. Monkeys will always be monkeys.

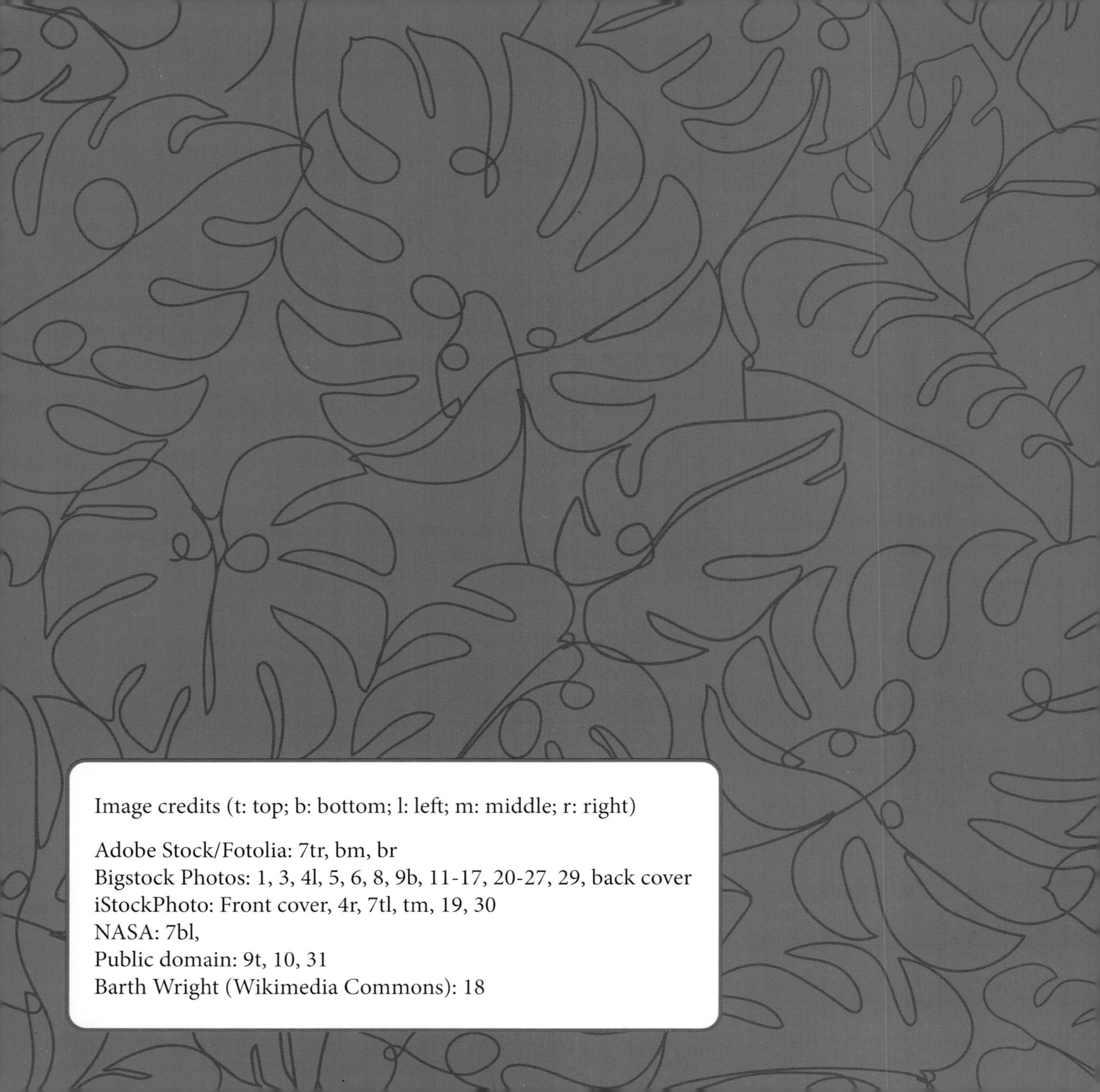

Image credits (t: top; b: bottom; l: left; m: middle; r: right)

Adobe Stock/Fotolia: 7tr, bm, br
Bigstock Photos: 1, 3, 4l, 5, 6, 8, 9b, 11-17, 20-27, 29, back cover
iStockPhoto: Front cover, 4r, 7tl, tm, 19, 30
NASA: 7bl,
Public domain: 9t, 10, 31
Barth Wright (Wikimedia Commons): 18